A Book of Verses

Edgar Lee Masters

LITERATURE HOUSE / GREGG PRESS
Upper Saddle River, N. J.

Republished in 1970 by
LITERATURE HOUSE
an imprint of The Gregg Press
121 Pleasant Avenue
Upper Saddle River, N. J. 07458

Standard Book Number—8398-1252-3
Library of Congress Card—77-104524

Reprinted from the original edition in the
Wesleyan University Library
Middletown, Connecticutt

A BOOK OF VERSES

A Book of Verses

BY
EDGAR LEE MASTERS

Chicago
Way & Williams
1898

CONTENTS

Contents

Contents

Contents

Contents

Contents

ODE TO AUTUMN

SEASON of gusty days and cloudy
        nights,
    The wind which showers wine apples
        to the ground
Blows at midday the long, pale, lunar
        lights
    O'er weedy fields with melancholy
        sound.
Summer has gone, but she has left a show
    Of downy clouds against the autumn
        sky,
Which the chill breezes chafe until they
        glow—

Ghosts of that luxury
Which now is by.

The golden trees against a sky of June
    Seem like a life that is too soon
        grown gray ;
Through smothering clouds the large
        autumnal moon
    Rolls argently her undiminished way.
The wonder of night's bright processional
    Abates not with the fading of the
        flowers,
Still glorious on all the earth doth fall—
    But for those withered bowers
    The pain is ours.

Here in my garden all the rich repose,
    The silence and the trance of summer
        eves

Has passed into a death presaging doze;
 The air is twinkling with the falling
  leaves
And sad elf-sighs do fill each little dell.
 Yet when the wind booms from the
  vale below
The moon is shaken like a cockleshell,
 Through the long, ragged bough
 That moans its woe.

If spring and summer be thy mask, O
  year,
 Which falls in autumn, leaving
  hideous
The thing we deemed was to our being
  dear,
 Then life may not be that it seems
  to us
In youth—but sometime may reveal—

When   the   worn   heart   the   shock
   can scarcely bear
A countenance to make the spirit reel,
   On reefs of keen despair,
   To perish there.

Ah, many a time and oft on nights like
   this
   The whip-poor-will has sent abroad
   her song
From depths of anguish and from heights
   of bliss.
   Now is it fancy?   But methought
   along
The   withered   fringes   of   the   tangled
   grass
   A few belated crickets sent a shrill
Of   hesitating   song—this,   too,   must
   pass;

Their little voices still
On mead and hill.

The night wind rises and the clouds which
    spume
    Dark from the faint and starry-
    lighted west
Are edged with fire against their heavy
    gloom.
    'Tis time that I should seek the
    thoughtless rest
Which day denies—much that we deeply
    prize
    Doth stir the mind's reflections and
    awake
The pains which else had slumbered—in
    such wise
    Rich, fruitful autumn, dear, for
    thine own sake

Through thy most fair disguise
We see Death's eyes.

A DREAM OF ITALY

DEAR heart, this leaf and blossom
    move
  Old hopes whose memory ne'er de-
    parts,
Plucked from dust that lies above
  The heart of hearts.

In our rough clime where skies are gray
  O'er leafless trees in winter's time
We dreamed of a serener day
  Through books of rhyme.

We saw the sky of Italy,
  We breathed the odor of its flowers,

And sailed o'er wastes of azure sea—
    The world was ours.

Since, from the lands whereto our ships
    In spirit sailed by wind and wave,
You send these frail and fragrant tips
    From Shelley's grave.

I turn to that dear hearth which knows
    Nor you, nor me, nor shall again,
And ask if aught before you shows
    By field or glen,

Great ruins, mountains, crystal lakes,
    Serenest seas or castled streams,
So bright as those our memory takes
    From our youth's dreams?

What glory lingers o'er that land,

Like that we saw in classic song,
With thought and fancy hand in hand,
  Far from the throng?

The shadow of our maple trees
  To Dante's voice was native too;
And Plato conversed here at ease
  The bright day through.

Now all we dreamed of lies before
  Your eyes, the past is now a dream;
I only hope that sea and shore
  Will take the gleam

From memory of those afternoons,—
  When all the world was true and
    fair—
Whose light was blent with rising moons,
  And fragrant air.

Men's hearts must crumble like the blooms
　　You sent, but from them may arise
The light that shall dispel the glooms
　　Of distant skies.

For genius throws o'er all this earth
　　The glory of a higher sphere,
And makes this humble flower worth
　　A noble tear.

AN INVOCATION

SWEET spring that brings the open
　　sky.
　　Fresh water and melodious wind;
And odors like the thoughts which lie
　　In souls grown better having sinned
Life springs anew within the heart,
Beneath thy smile—all lovely as thou art.

How trivial are the griefs we have,
　　How greater is our good than ill.
And even the singly cherished grave
　　So open to the winter's will
Is overgrown with flowers so fair,

Death is disrobed, and hope shuts out
    despair.

Breathe in our souls, dear mother earth
    The natural pleasure which is thine;
The sweet contentment and the mirth
    Which springs from strength, from
      peace divine.
Temper our lives to east wind and to west
And pillow us upon thy ample breast.

RELATEDNESS

ALL things are related, the inven-
tor's thought
   Has modeled the iron and shaped
   its form,
And lo, something new on the earth is
   wrought,
   And the blood of the millions is flow-
   ing warm.

And the poet who looks from his eagle
   height
   Has searched its meaning within his
   mind—
The simile, figure, the spiritual light
   Which gives a new hope to mankind.

29

WHEN UNDER THE ICY EAVES

WHEN under the icy eaves
    The swallow heralds the sun,
And the dove for its lost mate grieves
    And the young lambs play and run;
When the sea is a plane of glass,
    And the blustering winds are still,
And the strength of the thin snows pass
    In mists o'er the tawny hill—
The spirit of life awakes
In the fresh flags by the lakes.

When the sick man seeks the air,
    And the graves of the dead grow
       green,

Where the children play unaware
    Of the faces no longer seen;
When all we have felt or can feel,
    And all we are or have been,
And all the heart can hide or reveal,
    Knocks gently, and enters in:—
The spirit of life awakes,
In the fresh flags by the lakes.

THE WOOD

THE wood that echoed to our shout
   Is still with winter's loneliness,
Save when the Storm King is about
    With cries of strange distress;
The brook is frozen, the hill is bare,
And gray clouds fill the biting air—
    'Tis melancholy weather.

Yet dreary time shall we not say
Dark as thou art, that thou shalt stay?
For when the springtime comes again,
We shall not be as we were when
    We roamed the wood together.

32

IN THE VALE

L IKE some star-hidden lute whereon
  These wailing autumn winds were
     drawn,
This vale is magic, and the trees
Breathe to the air the melodies
Of dying nature's reveries.

The sunlight streams upon the wood,
But they are tuneless solitudes.
     And in the heavens near and far
     Like chariots driven on to war,
White clouds to mock the summer's mirth
Look down upon the faded earth.
     To what far heaven are they led
     Now that the latest flower is dead?

33

THE VISION

OF that dear vale where you and I
    have lain
Scanning the mysteries of life and death
I dreamed, though how impassable the
    space
Of time between the present and the past.
This was the vision that possessed my
    mind ;
Methought the weird and gusty days of
    March
Had eased themselves in melody and
    peace.
Pale lights, swift shadows, lucent stalks,
    clear streams
Cool, rosy eves behind the penciled mesh

Of hazel thickets, and the huge feathered
    boughs
Of walnut trees stretched singing to the
    blast ;
And the first pleasantries of sheep and
    kine ;
The cautioned twitterings of hidden
    birds ;
The flight of geese among the scattered
    clouds ;
Night's weeping stars and all the
    pageantries
Of awakened life had blossomed into
    May,
Whilst she with trailing violets in her
    hair
Blew music from the stops of watery
    stems
And swept the grasses with her viewless
    robes

Which dreaming men thought voices,
    dreaming still.

Now as I lay in vision by the stream

That flows amidst our well beloved
    vale,

I looked throughout the vista stretched
    between

Two ranging hills ; one meadowed rich
    in grass ;

The other wooded, thick and quite
    obscure

With overgrowth, rank in the luxury

Of all wild places, but ever growing
    sparse

Of trees or saplings on the sudden slope

That met the grassy level of the vale ;—

But nathless in the shadow of those
    woods,

Which sprinkled all beneath with fra-
    grant dew

There grew all flowers, which tempted
    little paths
Between them, up and on into the wood.
Here, as the sun had left his midday
    peak
The incommunicable blue of heaven blent
With his fierce splendor, filling all the air
With softened glory, while the pasturage
Trembled with color of the poppy blooms
Shook by the steps of the swift-sandaled
    wind.
Nor any sound beside disturbed the
    dream
Of Silence slumbering on the drowsy
    flowers.
Then as I looked upon the widest space
Of open meadow where the sunlight fell
In veils of tempered radiance, I saw
The form of one who had escaped the
    care

And equal dullness of our common day.

For like a bright mist rising from the
earth

He made appearance, growing more
distinct

Until I saw the stole, likewise the lyre

Grasped by the fingers of the modeled
hand.

Yea, I did see the glory of his hair

Against the deep green bay-leaves fillet-
ing

The ungathered locks. And so through-
out the vale

His figure stood distinct and his own
shade

Was the sole shadow. Deeming this
approach

Augur of good, as if in hidden ways

Of loveliness the gods do still appear

The counselors of men, and even where
Wonder and meditation wooed us oft,
I cried, "Apollo"—and his form dis-
      solved,
As if the nymphs of echo, who took up
The voice and bore it to the hollow wood,
By that same flight had startled the
      great god
To vanishment. And thereupon I woke,
And disarrayed the figment of my
      thought.
For of the very air, magic with hues,
Blent with the distant objects, I had
      formed
The splendid apparition, and so knew
It was, alas! a dream within a dream!

THE FIFTH ACT

THE viol is broke, and the sculptur-
ed vase it is shattered;
Wild winds make the flying curtains to
writhe at the door.
The bright star is lost and its golden
splendor is scattered,
And the loved face is seen at its wonted
place nevermore,
When the spirit is dull and dumb.

For I know that the ray of the star is
stopped in its flight
By the heavy darkness, through which
it must pierce, like truth.

Darkness conquers at last, and the scep-
　　ter belongs to night.
Lost is the wildness and lost is the sweet-
　　ness of blooming youth—
When the spirit is dull and dumb.

And the windows are darkened not,
　　though the sound of the wheel
Is a whirr that can scarce be heard as it
　　slowly turns;
And the strings are yet whole on the viol,
　　which no more feel
The electric touch of hope and of love,
　　whose music burns
The spirits of those not dull.

One day is the same, and one week is the
　　same with the rest;
Gray skies are as futile as fair, for the
　　soul, like a well

Deep down in the earth, of the heaven is
    baned nor blest.
It hath its own blackness; no light, save
    the light of hell—
When the spirit is dull and dumb.

And he who may chance to pass through
    the hall of life
Should know that the chamber is closed,
    if the tenant be there,
The issue unknown, and secret the scene
    of his strife;
But the door is ajar of the dead, or those
    whom despair
Has made dull the spirit and dumb.

Look within! for the goblet lies prone,
    and has spilled its wine
On the floor, and the lamp is a wreck,
    and its flame has died;

For the tenant is lost in his visions,
    which are not thine,
And Life sits sadly apart in tears, like a
    scorned bride,
For the spirit is dull and dumb.

SPRING

WHEN stars are moist as baby's
      eyes,
  And the warm south wind blows
  over the grass,
And through the blue and balmy skies
    Skeins of white clouds swiftly pass;

When sugar water freely flows,
    And chanticleer leads forth his brood,
And breaking stalks the farmer goes,
    And Mary doffs her winter hood;

When boys fly kites high in the air,
    And meadow larks nest in the plain,
And water-rushes spring, and wear
    A pale green from the tender rain;

When in the brown rust of the log
　　The violet shoots its purple flame;
And by the lakes the hunter's dog
　　Seeks the master's wounded game;

When the April moon is an Indian boat,
　　And lovers take the longest path;
And nightly sylvan whispers float
　　And every tree its Dryad hath—
Then spring has come, and you shall see
Pink blooms on the apple tree.

ODE TO NIGHT

ITHURIEL sun, thy bright wand is
That which takes away the bliss
    Of the phantom wandering free,
    Sporting in his liberty.
Morn, whose piercing argencies
Scatter, nestling under trees,
Shadows of Hesperides;
    Of the maidens, three in number,
And the dragon whose red eyes
    Never closed in slumber.

When the moon is climbing well
To her topmost pinnacle,
    Ev'ry hill, and lawn, and dale
    Sleeps behind a silver veil.

O'er the quiet landscape drawn;
Till the sun, waked by the dawn,
Gazes with his eyes of tawn;
    And when Cynthia leaves her cloud,
    Round Pan's feet the wood nymphs
        crowd;
Stepping, peering cautiously
To his dreamy minstrelsy.
    All is changed; they run away,
    Following Pan as best they may,
Gathering 'round him who sits down
Underneath a gnarled oak's frown,
    To hear the great god play.

Science like the sun's bright glare
Thou hast but the Cyclop's stare;
    Microscopic, which reveals
    Hill and valley bare, and steals
Ev'ry Dryad from its tree.

Moon that art romance!
Thou hast more of harmony
O'er this world, which is a dream.
Thou dost make an Arcady
Of each wood and stream.
Filled with satyrs, gods, and fauns,
Tripping o'er the shaded lawns.
Science, thou dost analyze,
Tales of earth and of the skies;
Thou wilt give us in return
Naught for that, which thou hast torn
From the human heart away
Till it aches with agony.

Ithuriel sun, thy bright wand is
That which takes away the bliss
Of the phantom, wandering free,
Sporting in his liberty.

LINES WRITTEN IN THE DES-
PLAINES FOREST

THE sun has sunk below the level
    plain,
And yet above the forest's leafy gloom
The glory of the evening lightens still.
Smooth as a mirror is the river's face
With Heaven's light, and all its radiant
    clouds
And shadows which against the river's
    shore
Already are as night. From some retreat
Obscure and lonely, evening's saddest
    bird
Whistles, and beyond the water comes
The musical reply, and silence reigns—

Save for the noisy chorus of the frogs,
And undistinguished sounds of faint
  portent
That night has come.   There is a rustic
  bridge
Which spans the stream, from which we
  look below
At Heaven above ; ' till revery reclaims
The mind from hurried thought and
  merges it
Into the universal mind which broods
O'er such a scene.   Strange quietude
  o'erspreads
The restless flame of being, and the soul
Beholds its source and destiny and feels
Not sorrowful to sink into the breast
Of that large life whereof it is a part.
What are we ?   But the question is not
  solved

Here in the presence of intensest
    thought;
Where nature stills the clamor of the
    world
And leaves us in communion with our-
    selves.
Hence to the strivings of the clear-eyed
    day
What take we that shall mitigate the
    pangs
That each soul is alone, and that all
    friends
Gentle and wise and good can never
    soothe
The ache of that sub-consciousness
    which is
Something unfathomed and unmedicin-
    ed.
Yet this it is which keeps us in the path

Of some ambition, cherished or pursued;
The still, small voice that is not quieted
By disregard, but ever speaks to us
Its mandates while we wake or sleep,
    and asks
A closer harmony with that great scheme
Which is the music of the universe.

So as the cherubim of Heaven defend
The realms of the unknown with flaming
    swords,
Thence are we driven to the world which is
Ours to be known through Art, who
    beckons us
To excellence, and in her rarer moods
Casts shadowy glances of serener lands ;
Where all the serious gods, removed from
    stress
And interruption, build as we conceive ;

In fellowship that knows not that reserve
Which clouds the hearts of those who
    wish to live
As they, in that large realm of perfect
    mind.

UNDER THE PINES

UNDER the pines
    Where the night winds
        Mourn for the world.
Where scarcely moon or star
Beams in the dark so far,
Where the dead leaves are whirled
        Under the pines.

Sweeter this voice than all
Instruments musical.
Come the bright visions flown,
Wraiths of the summer gone—
        Under the pines.

Spirits of air may pass
Over the withered grass,
Naught shall invoke the tune
Dead with the perished June.
         Under the pines.

Now that the mid-night reigns
How the wild wind complains
         Under the pines.
Ah could the heart but know
Aught of the life below—
         Under the pines !

A SONG OF COURAGE

NO cowards are we, though our way
    has been dark with the lion.
No sluggards are we, our hands from
    our cloaks we have taken.
We have striven and won all the
    heights worth the having and
    winning.

Our life is a grievous thing, and its
    moments of pleasure
Like dew all ablaze with the lightning
    outspread by the morning

Are heavy as lead on the wings of the
    infinite spirit.

Our hearts are as urns which are filled
    from the rivers of heaven,
And sealed with the powers of life, 'till
    death breaks the vessel
And the waters return to their source
    by the throne of Jehovah.

We reck not what thunders are stored
    in the clouds that are o'er us ;
We scorn all the lightnings concealed
    in the sheath of the darkness.
We pass—and no power can alter the
    trend of our beings.

Should we then regret what has been or
    fear what may happen hereafter,

We are part of the logic that travels
    from planets to atoms.
Whatever has been, it will be, though
    the nations deplore it.

The sky is above with its stars and the
    sounding sea is around us.
We drink in the souls of the dead, and
    live by the strength of the ages.
The life of the world is a growth, and
    each race of men stands up higher.

I know not why man should survive in
    another existence,
Nor why he should cease with the unfit-
    ting death that o'er takes him—
But if the gods strike they must lift him
    to aid them in heaven.

A PASTORAL SCENE

THE sunken sun has left a golden
      haze
  Above the boundless fields, and like
      a band
The rim of distant forests meets the gaze,
  A ring of ebony around the land.

There is no sound of bird or insect save
  The warbling of the robin all unseen
Amid the orchard's fastness where each
      wave
    Of wind brings scent of fruit and
      grasses green.

The farmer's dog, whose distant bark is
    heard,
        Welcomes the swain and gladdens
        his return.
He greets his children with a loving
    word,
        And cheerful candles through the
        window burn.

Hushed is the forest, rife with noise
    by day,
        Until the moon appears above the
        hill ;
When numerous locusts drone their
    changeless lay,
        And in the covert sings the whip-
        poor-will.

Lo! her bright disc already peeps
above
The upland meadow, and the even-
ing breeze
Springs on strong pinions from the
silent grove
And sets to whispering all the leafy
trees.

IN AUTUMN

THE day is dead, the moon is high
    A globe of fire in air.
The owlets whoop, the crickets cry
    In meadows brown and bare.
And heavy mists obscure the sky,
    Like thoughts of brooding care.

The dead leaves rustle where we tread,
    The winds are whistling low.
And all we loved too soon has fled
    Ere winter winds shall blow ;
And on yon tree to mock the dead
    Sits perched the sable crow

THE DEAD HEART

JUST as the summer dieth,
    When every flower is blown,
And by the wayside lieth,
    And every bird has flown !
So dies the heart, when sorrow
No more from joy can borrow,
And hope turns from to-morrow—
    And all the world is known.

With summer hardly ended
    A film of death comes o'er
The sky, and all things splendid,
    The bright sun gone before.

This is in sooth Time's fiat,
Where love and life ran riot,
Now color and sound are quiet,
 And low winds seek the shore.

Passive, but not forgetting,
 What pain hath bound our brows,
Sad, and yet not regretting
 Gay revel and carouse.
Naught shall the heart encumber
In days that Life shall number
She numbed its sense with slumber—
 And Life shall not arouse.

AN ETCHING

THE dull sky and the yellow meads ;
    And the stripped trees moan-
      ing in the blast.
The mind that thinks, and the heart
    that bleeds,
    The unborn day and the buried past,
And this gray Sphynx called Life.

THE MYSTERY

THE eternal mystery remains,
　　And we may never compass it.
Life turns and reaching out attains
　　The cold airs of the infinite.
　　And swiftly whirling scorns our wit,
Until a current forms to wend
Our steps along within its trend.

Who may unshred the magic lines
　　That keep his feet upon a way,
And search the spell 'till he divines
　　The inner motive of the play?

Cerberus keeps our steps at bay
Though Science glances full and free,
And Plutus taunts her with the key.

So Æschylos was wonder-eyed
　　In gazing on this warp and woof,
The while his muse forever cried
　　In hidden tones, some power aloof
　　Hangs o'er us, else the heavens roof
The earth for naught, nor life should feel
Immortal airs around it steal.

Poets and seers, Homer, Mohammed,
　　Felt the current underneath
This sea of time, whose tides are fed
　　By wonder of the transient breath—
　　That wanders from the shores of
　　　　death,

They felt, but saw as in a dream
The shore-ward movement of the stream.

Ever we tremble at the edge
        That bounds the eternal's sacred
        sphere.
High cliffs of frowning granite hedge
        That place of hope and fear,
        And unseen forces guide and steer
The ships to doom, or where they rest
Amid the Islands of the Blest !

A WISH

WHEN the trump of doom shall
sound
    Let me lie in peace thereof.
Sweet oblivion have I found
    Far removed from hate and love.
Who would wake to life eternal
    Hazarding his joy or woe,
When he rests from things diurnal
    Where the springs of Lethe flow?
Life that loved us not, has gone—
Shall we take up what is done?
Though the trump of doom be blown
Let me lie in peace below!

ALL IS FANCY

LET the form of beauty be
  Wrapped in fancy's mystery.
Look and dream, but wish no more
For the white sails far from shore.
For on board those sails are gray
With the ocean's breath and spray.
And the silken cord and tassel,
With the fierce winds forced to wrestle,
Are but coarsest ropes and black,
Fit to bear the tempest's wrack.

Dreams of Life gave you no grace—
Then you met her face to face.
Now you dream of Death, and he
Mocks your fondest revery.
Clasp His seeming form and find
All the pain you left behind.

ALMOST

KING Tippu Tib, a savage and no
       more
Walked all alone along the ocean's shore
And found a shell he had not seen before.

As lightning leaps from depths of dark-
       est night
A great thought filled his struggling
       mind with light
And overpowered him with its angel
       might.

For as he looked upon the spiral shell,

A wonder strong as truth upon him
    fell,
He held its meaning for an instant well.

The nodes which girdle it from year to
    year,
Record its growth into an ampler
    sphere,
"Ya ho" he cried unto his warriors near.

They raised the cry and ran to do his
    will
Who feared some strange event of sud-
    den ill
He held the shell and bade them all be
    still.

He held the shell and beckoned to each
    one ;

They pressed about to see what would
    be done
King Tippu Tib was dumb—the thought
    was gone!

THE MARTYR

IN an ocean of light, in an ether of life
    On the wings of the soul,
I have floated and flown from the sound
    of the strife,
    From the stress and the dole,
From the shadow of hate and the sombre
    eclipse
    Of the battle of pain;
From the vision of anger with pallid lips
    And the places of gain.

As our hearts were aflame with thy
words by the way
When we knew thee no more.
Ah! we burned for our love for the gift
of that day
When thy mission was o'er.
Through an ocean of light to the peace
of thy throne
With my passion complete,
Oh receive me and keep me forever thine
own
In rest at thy feet.

THE EVENING STAR

O EVENING star, not as in youth's
        brief glory
    Youth's joyous spirit rises rapt, elate
At thy bright vision, even as transitory
    As joy that clasps us in this earthly
    state—
Do I now greet thee as I did of yore,
Do I imagine, follow and adore.

Pass with the mystery of the early even
  To some far fairer sky we know
    not of—
Aye, so we dream—type of the hope
    which heaven
    Rescued for us with all the soul's
      deep love.
Earth that we prize fades wholly at a
    breath ;
My spirit quickened when I walked with
    death !

VULCAN

VULCAN, whose anvil blows
    Fashioned the warrior's shield,
Helmet and sword for those
    Who die before they yield,
Marvels of strength and skill,
Proof to the battle's ill.
    There amid fire and smoke
Patience was still thy Aid.
    God-like the hammer's stroke,
So all the instruments of war were made.

He who from year to year
　　Hammers his bronze to Truth,
While the world's satyrs jeer,
　　While sinks the fire of youth,
Conscious that through all time
There swings the mighty rhyme
　　Which will o'er all these forged
　　　　events prevail,
And all their harm—
　　He shall not fail,
Life's deeper logic animates his arm.

PSYCHE

KNOWLEDGE, thought, philos-
ophy
Our attendant angels be.
    As a moth of evening flies
    Where the brightest flames arise—
So our hearts aspire to thee,
Beauteous divinity.

As the sky bends o'er the earth,
    So thy power is on the spirit.

Thou hast filled the world with mirth,
    And with song for those who hear it.
As the sun draws floating stars
    There to melt into his bosom ;
As the subtle-winged airs
    Are impregned when bursts the
       blossom,
So our hearts aspire to thee
Beauteous divinity.

SAPPHO

CLOUDS in heaven frown, and the
     tide is flowing
Dark, and winds are loud round the
    promontory ;
Still, with wide eyes pensive o'er all the
    waters ;
     Sappho, thou lookest.

Bare the rocks and cold for the touch of
    shoulders,
Veiled no more from eyes, nor from bitter
    sea-winds ;
Now, small hands clasped tight, and
    with hair disheveled
     Death doth beguile thee.

Down beneath thy feet thy soft lyre has
    fallen,
Fallen there the coronal leaves whose
    edges
Touch the strings, and they to the winds
    make answer
        Faint, but how mournful.

Beauty, genius, fame, all of these the
    high gods
Gave to thee, reserving sweet love, thy
    passion
Scorn for love like thine cannot be for-
    given,
        Here, nor in Hades.

Who was he whose heart he could steel
    to music?
Made by hands whose touch was electric
    fire.

Star of song, why wert thou enthralled
    so fully,
        Thus of this Phaon ?

Thou whom we have sung in these sterile
    seasons,
Praised and loved made drunk with the
    sweet of thy song,
Thou whose stole we fain would have
    touched to render
        Homage and honor,

Thou wert scorned, unloved of this
    soulless stripling;
He was free to kiss on thy brow or
    tresses
He might sit and list to thy wondrous
    singing,
        Yet he was unmoved.

Thus at close of day with the breeze that
    follows,
Darkly o'er the waves, while behind the
    shadows
Spread and seek the base of the cliff far
    downward,
        Death doth beguile thee.

Vain is life and vain are all things when
    love is
All the heart desires, and is still beyond
    it.
Death will love when all have forsaken
    mortals—
        Sappho, thou knewest.

Far at sea a sailor descried a star fall ;
Sail and drift at last in the sea and
    perish ;

Fall and fade from sight as it were
   Hesperus
     Sunk in the waters.

Clouds far west are bright, and the tide
   is flowing ;
Round the cliffs the halcyons fly in twi-
   light ;
There, the lyre is stirred by the winds of
   heaven—
     Sappho is deathless.

TO A MOTH

SOFT phantom of the summer even-
tide,
From bowers of odorous dusk, thy
noiseless wings
Were closed in slumber when the day-
light died
In some rose garden where the cricket
sings;
Round whom spent petals charged with
summer fell
The lovliest harvest of all lovely
things.

Wherein, until the full moon's gorgeous
spell
Awoke nocturnal music in the grass,
And in the shuddering trees, that haunt-
ed dell
Of flowering bushes, and a fragrant
mass
Of leaves and tendrils, sheltered thy re-
pose.
Whence thou did'st flit to thy fierce
fate, alas !
Here in my lamp, whose bright allurance
glows,
A treacherous beacon, beaming out
afar,
As if it were thy soul's abiding star.

Like some full blossom driven by the
breeze,

From twilight and the regions of
 the West,
Lit by dim stars, as if untraveled seas
 Beneath stood tideless in unchang-
  ing rest;
Or, as if Egypt's level waste of sand
 Lay in submission of the Sphynx's
  breast,
Their eyes, these stars; thy mottled
 wings had fanned,
 O'er flowery lawns, the balmy air
  between.
Eager and palpitant to reach the brand
 Which was thy doom; as one who
  scorns the mean
'Twixt earth and heaven, lifting far too
 high
 His love unquenchable and ever
  keen

To some cold flame fixed in the windless
sky ;
It was with thee e'en as with us who
yearn
For vaster visions, and whose spirits
burn.

The risen moon floods valley, hill, and
plain
With crystalline splendor, and the
trees show clear ;
Yet thou art still from that brief fit of
pain,
Dead ere the summer, which made
living dear.
Through flame, the sepulcher from fabled
eld,
Of genius and of love, and all who
wear

The robe of beauty, and whose spirits
   held
      Converse with heaven;—miracle of
         hues,
The rapt intelligence which once pro-
   pelled
      Thy peacock pinions through the
         falling dews,
Slipped to a sleep whereof this summer's
   dream
      Is its dim dream, whose memories
         interfuse,
Of fragrant ways and glassy star-lit
   stream
      With frailer dreams, until thy fan-
         cied flight
      Glimmers away in some unvisioned
         night.

Yet it is beautiful to perish so;
  Ere the bright velvet of thy wings
    was marred;
Ere leaves do fall and frosty breezes blow.
  How sorrowful upon some lifeless
    sward,
I had beheld thee, lying stiff and dumb,
  The cold dew on thy wings. Like
    some great bard,
Who, living past his time of song, grows
    dumb,
  And still the figure of a perished past
Mutters of triumphs in a time to come.
  But thou, like those whose requiem
    was a blast,
Of deathless music quickening the pyre,
  Hast won death so, while every mead
    is grassed,

Tender and green, thy being's rapt de-
sire.
Teach us that youth and genius
brave his breath,
And grow immortal at the kiss of
death !

ILLINOIS

ILLINOIS, an empire is thine of billowy
   fields of glory,
Meadows of stretching green and
   forests whose depths are cool,
Hills that brighten in spring o'er rivers
   that tell a story
Of peace in the June-days mirrored
   in many a lucent pool.

Measureless miles of sunlight lie on the
   flowerful meadows,
Flamed with the clover blooms, with
   purple flags by the mere.

Deep in the maple woods is the silence of
  restful shadows,
Where the cry of the restless jay is
  joyful and clear.

Yes, if the whole world barred us, still
  the bountiful season
Would garner a foison of fruit and
  of golden grain.
Blessed is this land of ours, a stranger to
  nature's treason,
Which smiles 'neath the mingled
  graces of sun and rain.

Thine is a sturdy race, a bulwark in days
  of peril;
Whose children are fit for the field,
  or the hall of state.
Rich is this soil of mind, nor shall it ever
  grow sterile

While the great Republic thrills
with a sense of fate.

Here shall our epic thrive in the ages
hereafter:
Song of a noble race, its growth is
already begun.
All that was done before shall be food
for the high god's laughter—
The flower of Art is the child of the
soil and sun.

Here War is the thrall of Peace; give us
the epic of gladness,
The triumph and not the trial, the
victory of mankind;
Where Science has stilled the ghost of
the old world's sadness,
And Art is a glorious hymn of the
perfect mind.

NITOCRIS

NITOCRIS, Queen of Babylon, had
    cut
    Above the doorway of her granite
      tomb
Words of this import: "Keep these
      portals shut
    To all my great successors yet to
      come;
But haply, should his majesty have
      need
    Of moneys, he may open and with-
      draw
Such proper sums as fit the end. Take
      heed—
    This is the Queen's injunction and
      the law."

But when Darius broke the heavy
    gates
    And sought the treasure with un-
    holy hand,
He felt how base he is who violates
    Whate'er the dead may leave as
    their command,
And read these words: "Most wicked
    and profane,
    Most covetous and sordid, here to
    tread,
That thou should'st through a selfish
    greed of gain,
    Despoil and loot the chambers of
    the dead !"

THE LARK

IT was a little bird that sang for them
  Under an April sky;
And they heard the silver notes of the
  lark
  In a field of growing rye.
For the spirit of life is everywhere
  In the tender weather of spring.
And their love blossomed out like the
  reddest roses
  To hear the meadow lark sing.

100

Ah, greenest fields and flowering mea-
dows,
Under an April sky,
Love kindles the spirit of joy in the heart
And brings the tear to the eye.
April has gone and the summer is dying,
The lark should have taken wing,
For their hearts leap up with a sudden
pain
When they hear him sing.

ROMANCE

ROMANCE that loves the flower
    Best in its early bower,
White moons, the twilight hour,
    The morn, the eve;
Flies when the sun of thought
Through its frail surge has shot
Light, like the sand which wrought
    Gold through the sieve.

Once in this solitude,
Deep in this laurel wood,
A Grecian temple stood;
    Fair, chaste and high;

Its front entablature
The shapes of sea-gods bore,
One star hung o'er it pure
    In mellow sky.

Around, beneath, above,
Arose the songs of love,
The songs that stir, that move,
    That wake, that thrill;
The glancing laurel leaves
Shook with the summer seas,
Crinkled by midnight breeze,
    In star-light still.

No man might go within
Stained with the world's large sin—
Fair maids with raiment thin,
    Went in or out.
And men whose hearts could feel
Deep love for the ideal,

Whose faith no worlds could steal,
    Or stain with doubt.

But now the temple lies
Before its enemies—
They jeer, they satirize
    Its fallen state.
Likewise the laurel grove
Wherein all music throve,
The steel of sorrow clove
    And laid prostrate.

Where waved the blossomed bough
The villian drives the plough
The weighted cornstalks bow
    In sensual pride;
Where sang the nightingale
The crow and vulture rail;
Rent is the dreamy veil
    Which beautified.

WHAT YOU WILL

APRIL rain, delicious weeping,
     Washes white bones from the
     grave,
Long enough have they been sleeping.
     They are cleansed, and now they
     crave
Once more on the earth to gather
Pleasure from the springtime weather.

The pine trees and the long dark grass
     Feed on what is placed below.
Think you not that there doth pass
     In them something we did know?
This spell—well friends, I greet ye once
     again
With joy—but with a most unuttered
     pain.

WHEN LEAVES WERE SERE

WHEN leaves were sere, and
skies were dun
And birds were still, and snows begun,
And bright the Dog and Triple Tun
From Autumn's cloudy gale;
What time the stars arose and set,
There were rare bouts of winged wit,
When Johnson and when Shakespeare
met,
O'er cups of English ale,
Ah me,
O'er cups of English ale.

If candles since have burned as bright,
As then they did on many a night,
Yet wit was never since so light,
    Nor wisdom since so hale,
Ere we forget them, let us praise
The glory of those vanished days,
Their cordial cheer, their manly ways,
    Their cups of hearty ale,
      Ah me,
    Their cups of hearty ale.

CERES AND PROSERPINE

NOW Enna bathed in one vast sheet
    of light
Moved to and fro its sea of fragrant
    grass.
When Proserpine who led a blooming
    throng
Of maids fresh filleted with bare white
    feet
Came forth to gather flowers for her
    hair.
And while with shouts they ran now here
    now there

With flying stoles as white as summer
    clouds

A wondrous prodigy came o'er the
    scene.

For lo! a little crack spread near her
    step,

Which moving serpent wise grew long
    and wide,

And from it issued curls of purple
    smoke

Which thickened densely 'till a heavy
    cloud

Blotted the golden air.   Then from the
    gulf

Fire breathing steeds whose eyes were
    glowing coals

Yoked to a chariot of iron arose.

The visage of the charioteer was dark

Whose raven hair smote the retreating
    blast.

And 'round the spokeless wheels emit-
    ting sparks
Smoke whirled and clung as to a water-
    wheel
The falling waters circle into spray.
So was my loss accomplished, for at
    once
Amid the shrieks of her companions,
    she
Was carried in the chariot out of sight.
Now doth my longing lengthen with the
    days,
Soon will the echoes of the shepherd's reed
Bewitch my steps o'er meadow, hill and
    plain.
By night or day I'll follow on, or if
'Tis morn or noon, or if the humid
    night
Tranced with the sighs of ocean-tides
    make sweet

The dim, long ways. Or through old
    woods where sleep
The sprites of summer, I must take my
    way
Through silences that speak like tones
    of life.
But when young April weeps warm
    tears for me,
The gods know where, in wooded vale
    or where
High purple rocks are beacons for the
    flames
Cf daffodils, or by a cave, or near
Some slender brook, or on some gentle
    hill
My child shall clasp me with a long
    embrace.
As once reposing near the southern sea
Worn with regret and travel, she arose
Being released a season of her lord.

Then as her large fawn eyes looked into
    mine,
Joy of this meeting and restrained
    regret
For this strange doom that binds both
    her and me
A lark burst into song above our heads;
A shadow of mild green fell swift as
    light
On all the earth, and one strong sigh of
    wind
Charged with the smell of opening leaves
    and flowers
Blew through the tresses of my won-
    drous child.

RETRIBUTION

THE moon was a hornèd light,
    Around no cloud was seen,
And there in the wood the specter stood,
    That haunted St. Augustine.

For it rode a death gray horse,
    'Twas clothed in a flowing cloak
And it beckoned men to its mid-wood den
    In the shades of the giant oak.

None went—but wait you shall hear
    The tale as it should be told ;
For a man receives whatever he gives,
    Whatever he metes is doled.

One night when the moon was low
    And still was the hour and late
A man leaped forth from the under-
      growth,
    With a dagger of deadly hate.

And the man who rode a horse,
    All clad in a flowing cloak,
Was murdered there, ere he was
      aware,
    And hid by the giant oak.

But later the moon being low,
    When around no cloud was seen,
The murderer stood by the edge of the
      wood
    That bounds St. Augustine.

And sudden before his sight,
    A shape on a death gray horse;

And his limbs waxed stiff, and he felt
    as if
In the hands of an awful force.

Then it beckoned him with its hand:
    He would shout but he had no
      voice,
And he followed the dead, wherever it
    led,
    For he had no other choice.

He followed the specter on,
    And never a word was spoke
Till their steps were staid, where the
    corse was laid
    'Neath the boughs of the giant
    oak.

And there by the feeble light
    Of the horned and sinking moon,

The specter stood and raised its hood,
    And the man fell down in a swoon.

And the demons that lurked around,
    The horrors and all remorse,
Did choke his breath, to the land of
       death,
    And left his body a corse.

Since then no one has seen
    The specter there as of old,
For a man receives whatever he gives,
    Whatever he metes is doled.

THE VANQUISHED

I GRIEVE for those o'er whom the
heavy wheel
Has driven the car of carvéd silver
and gold;
With the speed of triumph, and the flash
of the victor's steel
Beating the conquered beneath the
ensanguined mould.

What! was the Persian King not as bent
on the prize
As the Greek who triumphed and
vanquished him from the sea?

117

Two thousand years and more yet his
spirit must agonize
    For our taunts and the pæans we
    raise for that victory.

And how could he who launched the
Phillippics rise
    So vastly great had his rival been
    common and mean?
Fools that we are, we forget him or else
we despise
    That the praise of the victor may
    keep his fame ever green.

Alas! for the spirit consumed in a fruit-
less cause,
    For the splendor of thought that
    destroys the thinker alone;
Was the heart of Hayne in the right for-
bidding a pause

To the fray with the lion of state
    who welcomed him on ?

Why howl ye that some have arisen
    where others fell ?
    For the Samsons who slay a tribe
      with an ass's jaw ?
For Achilles whose wrath sent the souls
    of unnumbered to hell
    And rose in his might, a figure for
      praise and eternal awe ?

I grieve for those who earnestly strove
    and failed,
    Who were either eclipsed or fell with
      the fall of a wrong ;
Whom the steps of death o'ertook ere
    the noon was hailed ;
    The revenge of the years, the shouts
      of the thoughtless throng !

THE WHITE CITY

THE autumnal sky is blue like
June's,
The wooded isle is sere below
Reflected in the still lagoons
    Beneath the full noon's brilliant
    glow.
Around the wondrous buildings show
    Their sculptured roofs and domes
    and towers,

Like Rome, ere crime had laid her low,
　　Ere the rude North's barbaric
　　powers
　　O'erwhelmed her art, which now
　　again is ours.

See the triumphal columns crowned
　　By Neptunes—see Diana there,
The tense bow ready to rebound ;
　　And Victory's wings are high in air.
See Liberty within her chair,
　　And over all the Republic stands,
With countenance serene and fair,
　　The staff and eagle in her hands,
　　Whom we adore, because she loosed
　　our bands.

And back of all the Peristyle
　　Protects the land against the sea,
And here the flashing fountains smile

And varied flags float full and free,
A solemn splendor which may be
    The presence of the majestic dead,
Reigns in the air until the knee
        Would bend in reverence, and the
            head
        Be bowed for truths we have in-
            herited.

Aye, truths and beauty and the power
        Which makes this vision all our
            own,
Though for a brief and passing hour;
        Aye, all which drove beyond the
            cone
Of light, of thought, the withered crone
        Old superstition.   Plato reared
Within the mind his burnished throne—
        But Bacon o'er the sea of knowl-
            edge steered

And sought out nature where all
    men had feared.

Then steam grasped ponderous wheels
    and drove
    The winged car from shore to shore,
And swifter than the thoughts of love
    The tense electric wires bore
Their freight of thought the long miles
    o'er,
    Till naught was hidden from men's
    eyes
Where all was miracle before,
    The earth lay conquered and the
    skies
    Unveiled themselves to man's great
    enterprise.

Then Justice shook to earth her chains
    Unfettered now to do her will;

And Liberty expunged the stains
  Of blood in centuries of ill.
The awakened earth shook off the chill
  Of darkness as her heart grew
    warm
To deeds of daring right, and still
  The nations fairer grew of form,
    In that great birth, the child of that
      fierce storm.

And thus where art and science hoard
  The trophies of the fruitful years,
The mighty spirits which out-soared
  The shadows of their trials and
    tears,
Dante's and Homer's and Shakes-
    peare's
  Seem hovering in the sun-lit air,
Now when the attentive spirit hears
  The first sighs of the year's despair,

While sorrow dyes the earth in hues
    most fair.

Hark! The Ave Maria rings
    From out yon fretted minaret
Enshadowed by the twilight's wings;
    Behold the golden sun has set,
Ten thousand lamps blaze in the jet
    Of water, shadowed nook, and tree;
Above, the stars again are met.
    This is a heavenly fantasy—
    Ah, that this dream should ever
        cease to be.

And lo! How white, how glorious
    These fanes and temples now ap-
        pear;
How pure a mood is now o'er us,
    The evening bell is sweet and clear.
And there by Dian's brow, how near,

A star shines singly and alone;
Right o'er the dome's symmetric sphere!
The flags against the sky are blown—
And all we cherished once is quickly
gone.

WALT WHITMAN

THE earth which gives and takes,
   Which fashions and unmakes
  Whate'er we prize
Has drawn unto her breast
The face which knew her best,
   The kindliest face we had and closed
    his eyes.
While Aeschylos and Job had gone
    before,

And all strong inspiration long was
    o'er
    He struck the harp to ancient
    melodies.

The great Republic's love
For which he pained and strove
    With might and sense;
Whereto he raised his song,
Which drives like leaves along
    Strong thoughts in storms of
    primal eloquence,
Grieves for him dead, and clips his flow-
    ing hair,
Decks with sweet flowers the place about
    his bier,
    For him who has departed bravely
    thence.

The soul of him who could

Find true in false, and good
   In everything.
From woman, man and boy
Learned all he knew, took joy
   In masonry and mines and house-
      building.
Like those Prometheus taught at wis-
      dom s birth,
Has floated from the shadow of our
      earth,
   To heights the mighty reach on
      dauntless wing.

The eagle eye, which saw
The spirit's worth, the law
   Of fairer fate
The Nation's final form
Through past and future storm,
   The fabric of a safe and gracious
      state,

Is closed by envious death, but not in vain
The vision he projected will remain,
    To be our life hereafter soon or late.

He knew these pageants pass
As in a magic glass
    And fill the shade
With substance, which before
Was empty, that no more
    Is reached than dreamed of, for
        which men have paid
In hopes and deeds, in virtue and in
        love,
In every noble thing man dreameth of
    In casting off despairs which on
        him weighed.

He was the truest child,
Our Western world beguiled
    And heaven bestowed.

Vast as our plains of wheat,
Sweet as our winds are sweet
  High as our mountains in the
    feathery cloud.
As strong as rivers flowing from the
    west,
Fruitful as California's sea-washed
    breast
  Broad as the land he made his loved
    abode.

He flung the past aside
The gods of field and tide
  Of hill and plain.
The green tree was his shrine
To him, all things divine
  The common road, small hamlets,
    drought and rain.
The Sun, which is Apollo, was his
    god,

Gave in his hand the gold divining
rod
  And said, I clasp the world and
    have no stain.

In seasons of despair,
In times of poisoned air
  He kept the faith
Of cheerfulness, of strength,
Of man's triumph at length,
  The love of life had given him love
    of death.
He stretched his hands, he could not
    know to whom,
With sandals of content he proved the
    gloom,
  Like fall's first sighs he gave away
    his breath.

There on the beetling heights,

Above our days and nights
    Our shade and shine.
He is enthroned serene,
The great of old between,
    The guardian of the land he made
        divine.
What though the great Republic
    grieveth sore,
For thee her bridegroom hastened on
    before,
    The pilgrim's bride will leave her
        hopes for thine.

THE TWO FOES

ONE had two foes as wakeful as the
    snake
  Intent upon its prey to do him
    wrong;
A man and woman who for hate's own
    sake
  Spread snares and scattered poison
    all along
The path they trod.   And while at first
    their deeds,
  Had no concert of plan, for neither
    mind
Knew of the other's hate, at last the
    seeds
  Each one was sowing crossed, as
    men may find

Some strange distortion spring from
    plants that grew
      Too closely, so their several hates
      gave birth
To one unholy passion when they
    knew
      The mutual thoughts that robbed
      each heart of mirth.

And as for him, though somewhat
    worn with age,
      The curse of Envy made each word
      he spoke
A venemous toad, and impotent with
    rage
      He raved, or into obscene laughter
      broke,
Seeking to overthrow the true and sage
      Who scorned his hate. And as for
      her enough

To chronicle the fate that to her fell;
　　For surely all her soul was turned
　　to love
Ere evil thoughts made inexpresible
　　Its dissonance, and fitted her to be
The boon companion of that hideous
　　. shape.
　　In short, they wedded, and his soul
　　set free
From their divided lives, could not
　　escape
　　Joy of revenge, in thinking that
　　these two
　　Must sting each other's spirits
　　through and through.

BYRON

THESE are the falls men name St.
    Anthony;
This is the mighty Mississippi's
    source
And I have watched with what
    tempestuous force
These torrents plunge and struggle to
    be free
Among sharp rocks their vexéd destiny.
    But where the waters of the gulf
    are hoarse
    Dim, vast, intent, this river takes
    its course
Still as the surface of a charméd sea.

There was a man of strong and passion-
    ate youth
    Clothed with the might of waters
    which o'er-leapt
    The bounds of time; and had he
    only kept
The streams of life which deepen toward
    the mouth
    Of the eternal sea, then had they
    swept
Flecked with a thousand stars of patient
    truth!

AFTER THE FIGHT: IN ROME

FORTH from the fading lights
       that lit the scene
Of gladitorial strife, the multitude,
Impetuously rushed, and I who
       stood
Somewhat removed, behind the wall's
       thick screen,
Paused 'till I saw an opening between
    The surging crowd. Then made
       my fancy good
    By stealing softly through, and all
       unviewed

Of those who watch me with familiar
mien.

How sweet it was to leave the City,
fly

From the oppression of the theatre;

The sanguine dust, the cruel crowd, the
stir

Of hateful passion, and the dying
eye.

Ah, neath my palm tree to lie thought-
ful here

Charmed by the planets of the mid-
night sky!

WHENE'ER THE SKY IS VERY DEEP AND BLUE

WHENE'ER the sky is very
deep and blue,
And he who lounges looking up
may see
Far 'bove the languid clouds, it
seems to me
That I must be unhappy 'till I woo
Sweet nature in no common mood, for
who
Hath never longed once more to
wander free
In olden woods, or with old com-
rades be

Or   childish   sweethearts   long   remem-
    bered too?
  The only sadness that this weather
    brings
Is that I cannot fully reach the joy
It should inspire—for if I were a boy
  Mem'ry   were   not,   and   all   these
    sober things
Could not distain the spirit or alloy
  The   pleasure   of   the   crickets'   mur-
    murings!

CHANT À MARS

WHEN March's breezes blow,
    Cool with the melting snow,
Fresh with the sun's new warmth that
    falls oblique;
The houses' corners groan,
And valleys give a moan
For things we find no more, where'er we
    seek.

In fields that sleep serene;
That show suspected green;

The winter's water in each hollow lies.
Wherein like castinets,
The frog its music sets,
To winds that rise and fall, and fall and
      rise.
Over the hills the clouds
Throw swiftly falling shrouds—
    Over the plain they follow swift as
      light.
The vexed sun glides between
The mists of shade and sheen,
    And hastens to his summer's glor-
      ious might.

Old hopes are now renewed ;
Fond fancies re-imbued,
    With sweetness of their prime, long
      past and gone ;
Old memories and dear,
Sound in the dreamy ear

Like tinkling bells upon a distant
    lawn.

What is the year ?   What we
Who know sùch ecstasy ?
    Who die with autumn and with
        spring revive ?
Winds, clouds, and sun, and rain ;
The wakening wood, the plain—
    'Tis very joy to be this day alive.

We sit this brook beside ;
Here where the winter died ;
    Where miracles of flowers and buds
        are wrought,
Through earth and heaven afar ;
Through things that seem, and are,
    Let Fancy shepherd mild and won-
        dering thought.

FLORA

On the Picture of Sandro Botticelli

THIS is the face of Flora—come
and look!
Her wild fawn eyes are gazing into
thine;
Her hair falls o'er her temples silken
fine
And round her neck; within its skeins
are shook
The blossoms of the spring which at one
strook
She oped and filled their eyes with
dewy wine.
And thus her gazing makes my
spirit pine,

146

For what it fancied by a little brook:—
  Once when the spring rose from the
    winter's trance,
  Yet slept as when the green buds
    first appear,
And new leaves start half shy between
    the leaves—
  Stretched in a wood, I saw this
    wild nymph peer
  With dreamy eyes at me, and that
    same glance,
Bred a sweet pain which Spring fore'er
    revives.

A FAIR PICTURE

HERE in this counterfeit of life
behold
All that begot the ancient bards
despair.
Who strove with art of cunning
song to share
With men to be their ecstacy, and sold
Life and the peace thereof, and hope of
gold
To keep in glory of rhyme her
wondrous hair,
And all her ways and looks that
she might fare

Haply and as she was in days of old.
    And so her face that makes a work
        of art
This fragile parchment wherein it is set
By grace of light and shadow having
        met—
    To rosiest flint its glory should
        impart
Carved carefully into a statuette
    Or have the treasuring of the lyrist's
        heart.

A WOMAN OF GENIUS

THERE was a golden flower whose
life was fed
By spiritual fire and dew and ten-
der air;
Held warm by starlight in a Dryad's
hair
Until the shadows from Hesperus fled.
Near by stood Himures with averted
head
From too much love, and now but
half aware;
Likewise high Hope and all shapes
good and fair.

Each waiting for her petals to be
spread.
Anon amid the crimson hues of
morn,
And delicate lightnings, as the Dryad
stole
For comfort in green leaves; the
west wind blew
The nestling petals free; and so was
born
Through all the gods' desire your won-
drous soul.
Which all men worship for their
love of you.

INGRATITUDE

PENSIVE amid these walls of beet-
    ling gloom
    After life's restless struggle, I am
      here,
    In Death's own land, beyond the
      flight of fear,
Void of all sound and sterile of all bloom.
For when the noise and clamor of life's
      loom
    Stopped suddenly, and Silence, like
      a mere
    Engulfed the roar of earth, my soul
      fell sheer

Down in the hollow of this changeless
    doom.

  Ah! derelict upon this shore,
    washed in

  By the last tide of fate, and like a
    shell

Re-echoing the tenor of the sea!

  I brood on this as my most grievous
    sin,

  That he who was my friend and loved
    me, fell

Through my ingratitude and treachery.

THE SOLUTION

AH! many times have I in some rapt
mood
Marveled that sage nor saint has
ever heard
Out of the infinite mystery any
word,
Whether of ill to mortals or of good.
For wandering often in the silent wood,
When anxious questionings and
sorrows gird
The eager heart, it feels its instincts
stirred
To audience of things not understood

In ages gone; wherethrough no voice
 cried yea
  To ease the terror of the perished
  years.
  And yet no message came; where-
  fore these fears,
Should hie them like the shadows from
 the day;
  This very silence all the mystery
  clears;
And naught is said, for there is naught
 to say.

DISCEPTRED

T HIS barren tree, dead, withered, which lifts high
    Its barkless boughs to heaven in appeal,
    Reminds me of that king who would unseal
The future by portentous birds which fly
O'er one lone peak—just as these twigs now sigh
    So sighed old Barbarossa, who could feel
    The past too deeply, longing to reveal

His presence in the strength of monarchy,
Yon points are perches for the screaming
jay,
The crow, the vulture, and the
hooded hawk;
The mild winds set them creaking—yet
what wars
They waged of yore when storms
abroad did stalk—
Disrobed, disceptred, robbed of life's
sweet day,
And sense of power beneath the glanc-
ing stars.

ON READING ECKERMAN'S CON-
VERSATIONS WITH GOETHE

SOME say that visioned men at
times have seen
Far down a dreamy vista which did
close,
With brilliant clouds, the topaz and
the rose.
The which did tremble gorgeously and
screen
From mortal gaze the shapes of gods
serene;
And looking thence entranced have
heard the doze
Of thunder music, and man's
deepest woes

158

From lips immortal, dream and thought
    between.
I too, have heard deep voices of that
    kind,
    And watched the distant halcyons
        wing their way
    Around one peak of Peace that
        pierced a day
Of clearest light, seen clouds and felt
    the wind
    From heights of thought, and heard
        its notes at play
Adown the Olympus of one matchless
    mind.

THE SPHYNX

AH, men have canvassed with their
    subtlest wit
  The cold face of the Sphynx, to
    learn what lies
  Within the far look of its lidless
    eyes—
Those wizard eyes that pierce the veil,
    and hit
The awful secret, while its lips are lit
    With scorn supernal, that we
    agonize,
    And hope and pray for that which
    ever flies
Beyond our utmost grasp to compass it.

Look o'er the level waste of Egypt's
　　land,

　　Thou symbol of the unattainable!

　　Still smile thy scorn, but know I
　　　　caution well

All men to leave thee to thy lone com-
　　mand;

　　For whoe'er seeks thy face his
　　　　thought to quell,

Thou fallest on, and crushest in the
　　sand!

NAPOLEON BEFORE THE PYRAMIDS

THE mightest form of late ambition
        met
    The ancient's sternest when Napo-
        leon stood
    Within the spell of that dim soli-
        tude
Which wraps the pyramids, when night
        has set
Her few, large, solemn stars enskyed to
        fret
    The cone of heaven. Twins of the
        same brood!
    For thou didst trample down the
        multitude

162

That fame might never more repay the
    debt
  In trumpetings for thee, for thy
    powers's sake.
Whilst these, disceptered by the monarch
    Death
Hoped haply they should rise up from
    beneath
  These piles whose rearing made ten
    thousand ache.
In different ways ye sought immortal
    breath,
  And found it for the sorrows ye did
    make.

AN ANCIENT JURIST

THERE was a jurist in the days of
    old
    Whom grace of Fate made judge, it
      was a pity!
    Some said that he was learned in
      Coke and Chitty,
And therefore had a right to roar and
    scold
And babble in a manner manifold.
    So that the rumblings of a noisy
      city
    Scarce drowned his voice, he was so
      very witty,

Tempestuous and blustering and cold.
This legal Vulcan let the hammer drop
From day to day and fashioned
strange decrees,
And made all suitors very ill at
ease
Because he roared and found no way to
stop.
A wag at last stuck up such words
as these:
"This is a court and not a boiler-shop."

A VISION OF ART

AH Flora, of blue eyes and throat
so slender,
And brows as lustrous as the driven
snow;
When the carved doors of fancy
open go
I see thee there in robes of brilliant
splendor.
This is strong vision, for at most some
tender
Mood of an afternoon enwraps me
so
That 'tis thy presence o'er my
thoughts which flow

As visionless as those which stringed
    notes render.
In thine own Temple Art preserves
    her treasures,
Pale busts and vases and a Japan jar,
Full of spiced leaves, a careless lent guitar,
    A polished floor where tiger rugs
    are strewn.
Upon the lawn a marble fountain
    measures
    The happy hours beneath a sky of
    June.

AFTER THE RAIN

COME, for the soul of music is
    awake,
  The breeze is up, the azure sky is
    bare
  The twinkling leaves are sparkling
    in this air
Of glory and within the fragrant brake
  The quail calls, and around the
    meadowed lake
  A numerous flock of singing black-
    birds fare.

All choristers that in the lightings'
    glare
Kept silence in the trees, are forth to
    take
The freshness that has followed from
    the storm.
    Wrecks of the cloud are sailing in
    the breeze,
And in the flashes of the evening sun
    The genii of the air shake from the
    trees
The jewel water drops in which they
    swarm
And the half-moon floats in her sea
    pearl-wan.

LIFE'S SOLDIER

L IFE'S soldier brave, in moods both
  grave and gay
You watch the drama where the
  actors pass
Swiftly and vague like shadows
  o'er the grass.
And see the varied movements of the
  play,
Started at morn and finished in a day.
  Here do we look as through a dark-
    ened glass
  At friend and foe amid the strug-
    gling mass,

And the vexed spirit beaten and at bay
Frowns and reflects.   But often do
we feel
The under current, and the deeper
thought
Seems ever as it would unveil its
form.
So amid duties you shall not conceal
Your mood of listening to the music
wrought
Above the thunder of the city's
storm.

APOLLO AT THE PLOW

(Chatterton to his Friend)

FAITHFULEST and dearest of
the friends I have,
Forgive me for the weakness which
I show,
That while youth is, its nerve, its
spur, its glow,
Are quite consumed. Forgive me if I
crave
A deep repose, aye even in the grave,
Forgive me, that the fires of hope
burn low,
Condemned to ignominious steps
and slow
'Mong ravin' wolves within a prison
cave—

If you could see me now. But what
    I was
Thou   knowest   well—and   from   thy
    memory
    Ambition's   shape   will   rise—then
    quickly pass
    To me the Sampson of these grind-
    ing days,
Apollo plowing lorn and ruefully,
    His harp abandoned in the flower-
    less ways.

BALLADE OF SALEM TOWN

WHERE is the inn of Salem
Town
Where Lincoln loafed ere we knew
his name?
When the Clarys from Prairie Grove
were down,
And he kindled mirth with his wit
like flame.
Loud are these things on the lips of
fame,
But crumbled to dust is the log-wood
wall,
And perished alike are 'squire and
dame—
The toiling year is the Lord of all.

Where is the mill of such renown?
    And the sluice where the swirling
        waters came?
And the hamlet's sage and the rustic
        clown
    And those who had glory and those
        who had shame?
    And those who lost in this curious
        game;
The bully, the acred-lord and his
        thrall—
    Gone are they all beyond Time's
        reclaim—
The toiling year is the Lord of all.

But when jest passed 'twixt laggard
        and lown
    And the cold wind whined at the
        window frame,

Then careless alike of smile or frown
    He builded for those who should
        carp or blame,
    Thereafter when Error should seek
        to maim
The hand of Liberty in her hall,
    When he made Malice and Treason
        tame—
The toiling year is the Lord of all.

ENVOY

Prince! this shaft of marble is brown
    Ere a cycle is past, and at last will
        fall
But fame has fashioned his fadeless
        crown
    The toiling year is the Lord of all.

BALLADE OF SOCRATES

YE men of Athens, list to Socrates,
    And mark me how the Delphic
        oracle
Hath stripped me of the robes of joy
    and ease
    The price of those who triumph
        and excel.
    And stung my soul with questions
        which impel
My test of men who coax the tongue of
    fame.
I have had nothing but a world of
    blame
    Much sorrow and deep bitterness of
        heart

Some strange misgivings and the gift of
    shame—
  And yet, oh life how sweet and dear
    thou art.

Devoid of those accomplishments which
    please
  With little skill in love, it so befell
I won my wife Xantippe, greater tease
  Than these hard questions, harder
    far to quell.
  But having seen how baneful is
    love's spell,
More dread than Circe's making men her
    game,
And that a wife's tongue is a subtle
    flame,
  A whip of steel, a goad, a poisoned
    dart,

I have known all things which the god
can claim—
And yet, oh life, how sweet and dear
thou art.

I have searched out all men's philoso-
phies
And I have known all things
desirable,
And by the calm eternity of seas
My spirit conversed with Poseidon's
knell.
Through strife and grief I kept my
patience well,
Through noisy folly, insolent acclaim.
I have known all that men can think or
frame,
Hope for, aspire to, suffer or
impart—

Vexed with the heavy question whence
  we came—
  And yet, oh life, how sweet and dear
  thou art.

ENVOY

Great Zeus! thou knowest men despise,
  defame
My search for truth and beauty, and
  my name.
  Thou knowest also that our days
  depart
In vanity fore'er beyond reclaim—
  And yet, oh life, how sweet and dear
  thou art!

BALLADE OF THE STAGE

AN hour before the glowing stage
    We watch the actors come and go
Within the mimic equipage
    The hero, coward, friend and foe.
    The curtain falls anon, and lo!
Famed Athens looms above, perdie,
    The world's great theme of joy and
        woe—
Holds thought and revery in fee.

The time of sophist and of sage
 Who sought the future to fore-
  know,
Of knight and vassal, squire and
  page,
 Whom death with all of theirs laid
  low,
 Bequeathing to the stage to show
Whate'er they felt of grief or glee,
 By which the soul of man should
  grow
Holds thought and revery in fee.

Ah! where are those whom sacred rage
 Made life a torture doubly slow?
Whose fire of spirit lit the age—
 Who mocked death's seeming over-
  throw?
 The play of man went to and fro;

They saw and vanquished fate's decree —

   For all their genius did bestow
Holds thought and revery in fee.

ENVOY

Prince, we shall live in Art, although
   Death comes to set our spirits free.
And he who lies beneath the snow
   Holds thought and revery in fee.

BALLADE OF SAM JOHNSON

"He was kind that night"
—Boswell's Johnson.

ONCE when the festal board was
    merry
With sparkling wine and with
    Johnson's jest
The loud sage smiled and was gracious,
    very
Even to Boswell's wakeful zest.
The Chronicler's memory held this
    best

184

For lo! the satirist was polite;
    And wrote it out on his palimp-
        sest—
Ah but Johnson was kind that night!

Boswell the taker of notes was wary
    Since Johnson in sudden wrath ad-
        dressed,
A shaft of scorn which no wit could
        parry
    The barbs whereof Time could but
        divest.
    And Boswell taking therefrom
        unrest
Traveled o'er sea like a sorry wight
    And found at last the boon of his
        quest!
Ah but Johnson was kind that
        night!

Nectar, ambrosia, Tom and Jerry
 What they tippled no man has
  guessed;
Ruddy port wine or golden sherry
 Boswell's pages fail to attest.
  The board was joyful 'tis manifest—
All else suffers in Time's despite,
 For the scar was cured in Boswell's
  breast—
Ah but Johnson was kind that night!

ENVOY

Sam, how vain did you make protest
 And heap on Boswell many a slight.
Still he preserved your great bequest,
 Ah but Johnson was kind that
  night!

ST. MARY'S

FAIR eyes the shrines of dreams,
    The heavens of love;
Bright hair whose splendor gleams
    Thereout above.
Within the cloister arch,
She holds a spray of larch
    The day is hers and all the joy
      thereof.

Ah Clio all thy soul
    Is fully gone

Within the carven scroll
    Thou gazest on.
Be not so thoughtful wise,
For one with tender eyes,
    Looks to forget o'er all the level
    lawn.

Through drooping trees that stir
    And scarce suspire
The sky looks in to her
    The day's pale fire;
The fountain's rainbow mist,
The rose, the amethyst,
    The happy field that feels no more
    desire.

If bright clouds float above,
    And throw bright shade
Throughout this laurel grove

Where she hath strayed;
When all the day is still,
What sorrow scorns her will?
    What thoughts, what dreams, that
        can not be allayed?

'Tis June, the rose is full
    And water flows;
Whate'er is beautiful
    With her arose;
Fresh   morns,   and   bounteous
        noons,
Large planets, argent moons,
    White hours whose pluméd wings
        regret to close.

Yet, Clio, piteous voice
    Of all our deeds,
Her heart cannot rejoice

Whene'er she heeds
The scroll, almost complete,
Closed book of days most sweet,
 Dear words, that grow more dear
  the while, she reads.

The painéd muses gaze
 Seeing how near
The end is of school days
 For Julia here;
Melodious Greek, romance,
Light, laughter, dream, the dance:
 Smooth, golden thought that comes
  through many ways.

Dark eyes, the shrines of grief,
 The heavens of thought;
Regret hath no relief
 For days out-wrought.

Down from the cloister arch,
She drops the spray of larch,
The sun is sunk, and still is every
leaf.

IN CHURCH

The passion of the organ's breath
    Comes over me;
The resurrected life, the death,
    The agony.

The fair light through the purple panes
    Is purple too,
The spring wind's music swells and
      wanes,
    The window through.

The air is filled with hues, with scent
    Too faintly sweet,
Like souls that rise, where they were
    bent
    From Jesus' feet.

I have strange heart for prayer and
    hymn,
    For stoléd choir
They blend unto my spirit's utmost rim,
    In my desire.

The deep expressions of earth's love
    Become all mine,
Of individual grief, they move
    All thoughts divine.

To her of fairest face and even
    Of fairest name,

The divine of earth and heaven,
    Are one, the same.

Be this my plea—Her spirit is
    In all the air.
She is the flower, the organ's bliss
    The holy prayer.

If she were spirit all, descended
    From realms divine,
Her spirit were no further blended,
    To one. with mine.

Yet if her life had slipped away
    She were more dear;
Dear souls of heaven to whom we
      pray,
    To whom draw near.

But earth forbids much, whence much
    grief
  To us who live;
Ah for the long dreamed-of relief
  That hope can give.

Or else that she should be en-
    sphered,
  A golden star,
By death, a beacon thrice endeared
  To me afar;

A star, a holy hope, a guide,
  A saint, a shrine;
A tender heart, on earth denied.
  In turn for mine.

*   *   *

All songs are sung, the latest note
    Has died away;
From hues which o'er the chancel float,
    We pass to-day.

And she of fairest face and even
    Of fairest name,
The divine of earth and heaven,
    Are one, the same.

THE SEA

Βῆ δ᾽ ἀκέων παρὰ θῖνα πολυφλοίσβοιο θαλάσσης

Iliad Book I

I WHO am inland born, have some-
    times heard
  The sea's deep voice—a momentary
    wail
  When high waves rise and fly before
    the gale
And dash upon the beetling cliffs that
    gird
His wide domain; or with the fancy
    stirred,
  Seen at the sun-light's edge a glit-
    tering sail
  Under a sky serene and brightly
    pale
O'er darkling tides where wheeled the
    sad sea-bird.

But when I peering from the lonely
    shore
    Shall gaze upon the waters dancing
        free,
Then I shall feel like him on Mount
    Nebo,
    Or like the myriad shouting loud
        "the sea,"
Or like the gray priest, in his silent woe,
Who walked and heard their many
    voices roar!

YES, WHEN THE BLEAK STORM BLEW

YES, when the bleak storm blew
    Gray cloud and mist,
Young Love took wing and flew,
    Scorned and unkist.

False joy, the seneschal,
    Shouted him forth,
Shut from the rosy hall,
    Out to the north.

Then while the dancers gay
    Heard the bassoon—
And all the orchestra
    Warmed into tune.

Was he incensed, did he
  Pine in the wold
Blanch in the north winds' dree,
  Bitter and cold?

Nay, for the April came
  Mild air and rain
Touched into flowerful flame
  Valley and plain.

But 'round the door there grew,
  Never a bloom.
Drear was the house to view,
  Gray as a tomb.

False joy, the seneschal
  Wept at the door,
Vain were his tears and all—
  Love came no more!

HELEN OF TROY

On an ancient vase representing in bas-relief the
flight of Helen.

THIS is the vase of love
    Whose feet would ever rove
      In fragrant ways;
Whose hopes forever seek
Bright eyes, the vermeiled cheek,
      And cloudless days.

Though we do understand
Why thou didst leave thy land,
      Thy spouse, thy hearth;
Yet for thy self Greek art
Hath made our heart thy heart,
      Thy mirth our mirth.

201

For Paris did appear
Curled hair and rosy ear
    And tapering hands.
He spoke—the blood ran fast,
He touched, and killed the past,
    And clove its bands.

And this, I deem, is why
The restless ages sigh,
    Helen, for thee.
Whate'er we do or dream,
Whate'er we say or seem,
    We would be free.

We would be free from strife
And all the pain of life,
    And all the care;
We would find out new seas,

And lands more strange than these,
 And flowers more fair.

We would behold fresh skies
Where summer never dies,
 And amaranths spring.
Lands where the halcyon hours
Nest over scented bowers
 On folded wing.

We would be crowned with bays
And spend the long bright days
 On sea or shore;
Or sit by haunted woods
And watch the deep sea's moods,
 And hear its roar.

Beneath that ancient sky

Who is not fain to fly
     As men have fled?
Ah! we would know relief
From marts of wine and beef,
     And oil and bread.

Helen of Troy—Greek art
Hath made our heart thy heart,
     Thy love our love.
For poesy like thee
Must fly and wander free
     As any dove.

FAREWELL MUSES

HO! Muses nine,
  If one be mine,
Should I then pine
    For all the rest?
Nay, under my vine,
I'll sip my wine,
And herd the swine—
    And forsake the quest.

For each man's breast
Hath a bard for guest
And ah! 'tis best
    The bard should die.
Who heeds his behest
Will reap life's jest,
And the thorn hath pressed,
    Where his heart would lie.

And ye who buy
Men's souls with a cry
To fame while ye fly
 The clasp they need;
It is vain to vie
With gods who deny,
And over you high
 The gods have heed.

They have decreed
Each word and deed—
You shall but feed
 The sacred flame,
And those you lead
With a syren reed
Will wish them freed
 From your evil claim.

No win a name

Is a worthy aim;
And how free from blame
    Are the laurel leaves.
But 'tis a game
Where the swift get fame
And the slow have shame
    And the weak heart grieves.

But all spent sheaves,
My Muse retrieves,
She fashions and weaves
    With wheatless straw.
Whilst ye were thieves
Of my days and eves—
So my bosom heaves
    For Themis—the law!